Subversive Verse

A collection of poems about corporate cruelty, gender grievances, supreme shambles, political perversion, and race relations.

Also by F.I. Goldhaber:

Pairs of Poems

Ticket to Faerie

Stranger Than Fiction

Rebellion

Evolution

Chasing Time

Dragon Treasure

Firestone

To Rise Again

Finding Magic

http://goldhaber.net/

After more than three decades, storyteller and poet F.I. Goldhaber continues writing professionally. As a reporter, editor, business writer, and marketing communications consultant, she produced words for newspapers, corporations, governments, and non-profits in five states.

She wins awards for her fiction and poetry. Preditors & Editors readers poll ranked her second poetry collection, *Pairs of Poems,* third internationally. Various organizations honor her erotica works. Her short stories, novelettes, poems, news stories, feature articles, essays, editorial columns, and reviews appear in magazines, ezines, newspapers, calendars, and anthologies. She also published five erotica novels under another name.

In addition to paper, electronic, and audio publications, F.I. shares her words at events in Salem, Keizer, Portland, Seattle and on the radio. She appeared at venues such as Wordstock, Oregon Literary Review, bookstores, libraries, and Chemeketa Community College; gives presentations on subjects as diverse as marketing, writing erotica, and building volunteer organizations; and taught Introduction to Indie Publishing at Portland Community College and as a weekend intensive.

http://goldhaber.net/

F.I. Goldhaber

Subversive Verse

We the People of th
insure domestic Tranquility, provide for the common defense

Best read aloud.

Table of Contents

Subversive Verse

Political Poetry Publishing

ISBN: 978-1-937839-19-2

This book is a work of fiction. The names, characters, places, and incidents are products of the writer's imagination or have been used fictitiously and are not to be construed as real. Any resemblance to persons living or dead, actual events, locale or organizations is entirely coincidental.

Political Poetry Publishing
P.O. Box 80766
Portland OR 97280

Combating
Corporate Cruelty

Corporations

2005

Cellular One, Ford, U-Haul
Verizon, AT&T, American Express,
Hewlett Packard, U.S. West, MCI.

Corporate behemoths who have
crossed me, refused to do the right thing,
ignored the fair and just complaint.

I took you all on. I know who to call.
I know where to write. I use my words to battle
those who routinely abuse consumers.

FCC, FTC, SEC, PUC.
AG's Office of Consumer Fraud.
Familiar with the government alphabet soup,

I enlist their aid: for the threat of regulators
gets your attention. I work my way up from
supervisor to VP to CEO. Understanding corporate

structure — how to read annual reports — helps
pave the way. I count my victories
in dollars returned, letters of apology, payments made.

F.I. Goldhaber

Lincoln was a Republican

2007

If honest Abe had come to Oregon
to serve as Governor in forty-nine
how differently would our world have evolved?
Would corporations have gained the power

to corrupt the government? Would the man
elected instead to the White House have
antagonized the south and then fought to
preserve the union, trying to keep two

disparate cultures/economies
connected? Would all red states now belong
to the CSA? Without Texas as
spring board would Connecticut-born GW

have stolen two elections? Would we fight
now in Iraq or would 9/11
never have happened 'cause Haliburton
would have no power? Would the slaves in the

south have revolted against white owners
taking possession of the land they had
worked for centuries, perhaps with support
from a northern neighbor with states of blue?

Wallet Politics

2008

Put your wallet where your politics are.
You railing against Halliburton and
the war in Iraq and Afghanistan;
you complaining you can't find a job that
pays you enough to take care of your kids;
you upset by the lack of health care here;
you shop at Wal-Mart?

But, you say, goods at the other stores cost
so much more; you would have to drive further;
they have everything you need in one store.
Put your wallet where your politics are.
Pay attention to the stores where you shop.
Do you know where their merchandise comes from?
China? India?

Are their toys covered in lead? How many
children lost fingers making those sneakers
earning a dollar a day in sweatshops?
How can you spend money at a store that
destroys local business, deflates wages;
whose employees are eligible for
food stamps, Medicaid?

Can you justify saving your money
when you know it comes at such a high price?
Whose pocket do you pick when you choose the
cheapest source? And which politicians will
get campaign contributions from such firms?
Anyone you'd vote for, who represents
what *you* believe in?

F.I. Goldhaber

Cables

2008

I couldn't help but laugh
when I read about the
cables cut by anchors.

All the companies that
sent their jobs overseas;
laid off employees here

by the tens of thousands;
who said they had to move
facilities offshore

to stay competitive.
They'd no Internet or
telephone connections.

Under the ocean's surf,
disturbing the sea life,
fiber optic cables

bind the world together
with communication.
But carelessness caused

the loss of contact with
their underpaid Chinese
and Indian workers.

Trade Deficit

2009

Car after car passes
empty, headed for ships
to carry them across
the Pacific. They will
return loaded with trade
deficit: video

games, computers, cameras,
phones, television sets.
We buy Asian imports
and then wonder why we
cannot find decent jobs.
Only minimum wage

work pushing the products
that come in on rail car
after rail car. Loaded
with cargo containers
that go from ship to train
to truck to deficit.

F.I. Goldhaber

Corporate Repression

2014

I may not call it censorship, for
it's corporations not government
that refuse to sell my words, blocking
my work for violation of what
I must call out as arbitrary
and capricious "guidelines" that have no
basis in most jurisdictions' laws.

Those corporations decide what you're
allowed to read, to watch, and to think.
You may find my work offensive, but
do you believe you have the right to
prevent other folks from reading it?
And, what if someone finds the books you
love objectionable and burns them?

Gender Grievances

F.I. Goldhaber

Separation of Church and State

2010

"Congress shall make no law respecting an estab-
lishment of religion."
From First Amendment of U.S. Constitution

One of this country's founding fundaments,
is the separation of church and state.
A civil union, marriage brings hundreds
of legal rights, responsibilities,
established by filing certificates
with **government** entities. There is no
"sanctity" involved, just a business deal.

Men invented marriage to protect their
property. Throughout the millennia
marriages aligned countries, preserved trade
relationships, enriched nobility.
In some countries if you have religious
rites, you must have civil ceremonies
as well to obtain legal benefits.

All laws should apply equally to all
U.S. citizens. The constitution
has no provisions to deny rights or
privileges based on one's sexual
orientation. We need church and state
separate. Allow **everyone** civil
union certificates and benefits.

Individual churches can decide
who may have religious ceremonies,
but those should provide **no legal** standing.
Any who want the tax and civil rights,
must go through the civil process. Dump the
word marriage, let the churches have it, but
without denying anyone their rights.

F.I. Goldhaber

T

2014

Yes, you can marry now
and reap the benefits
of tax deductions, joint
adoption, judicial
protections, medical
privileges, and support.

But marriage rights mean little
to those who can't walk down
the street without fear from
hostility, assault,
panic if they need to
pee when away from home;

When their boss can fire them
with impunity if
he discovers their birth
certificate gender
doesn't match the one
that defines who they are.

And the hate hurts more when
it comes from those who share
the acronym, who should
remember what it's like
to live in fear because
"normal" doesn't fit you.

But all too often, the
L and the G forget
about the T at the
end and are first in line
to hurl invectives and
demonstrate their contempt.

Supreme
Shambles

F.I. Goldhaber

Five Old White Men

2014

Five old white men in their black robes sit
in Washington eviscerating
the bill of rights: an Uncle Tom and
oreo, a corporate stooge and
his clone, a lech, and racist members
of the forced pregnancy proponents.
Religious pretenders ignorant
of science, adrift in a world of
technology they still can't seem to
comprehend. Wined and dined by special
interests, embracing infectious
scourges of partisan politics
that erode the little prestige left
to the court and American faith
in the law. They surround themselves with
like-minded law clerks, consume only
media reports that reinforce
their opinions, speak exclusively
to audiences predisposed to
be sympathetic to their viewpoints.
From October through July they hand
down decisions gutting laws that once
protected rights of women, voters,
workers, and minorities. For a
monetary gain, they handed the
country to a man who did not have
the votes, sending U.S. spiraling
into recession. They made Orwell's
vision come to life by allowing
the NSA free reign, turning our
government into Big Brother. Time

after time, these millionaires decide
business privilege trumps people's
freedoms allowing corporations
to buy elections, deprive us of
health care, deny us the right to sue.
Now police invent more egregious
pretexts to arrest you because those
men give them carte blanche to search
every inch of your body inside and out.

Political Perversion

Winds of Change

2007

Nestled in the once safe valley
we listen to dire predictions
warning us of hurricane-force
winds never experienced here

before. Now the gale tears at the house
trying to rip away flimsy
shingles and brittle siding. The
current White House resident would

have us believe that climate change
does not concern us. But I see
drought become commonplace in the
lush valley and fires develop

into a ritual every
summer extending into fall.
I read of melting glaciers, of
starving polar bears, of islands

that disappear into the sea.
But, I only need listen to
the wind to know the truth of what
we`ve done to this world where we live.

F.I. Goldhaber

Oppression

2008

U.S. citizenship
will endanger your health.
In the republic where
we live, the rich govern
the poor. Did someone fool
you into believing
the U.S.A. is a
democracy? Never.

In France, the government
fears the people. Afraid
of protests, parliament
provides health care for all.
Thirty-five hour work weeks,
month-long vacations, and
free education keep
citizens off the streets.

In the U.S., people
fear their own government.
Saddled with college debt,
one medical crisis,
even just one paycheck
away from homelessness.
We live in terror of
losing jobs, getting sick.

Even employed, the odds
don't favor access to
health care. And hospitals
routinely dump those who
don't have insurance on
the sidewalk in front of
the mission or send them
off to die somewhere else.

We started the ball of
democracy rolling,
but they kept it in play.
Their citizens live free;
ours demoralized and
too frightened to protest.
Educated, healthy,
folk are hard to govern.

Keep them debt ridden, sick
ignorant, and poor and
they'll never cause trouble.
One percent own eighty
percent of the world's wealth.
Politicians do not
represent the people,
just the corporations.

Instead of fixing the
system to meet the needs
of the citizens, they
manage the people to
fit the faulty system.
Keep people hopeless and
pessimistic and you've
no worries 'bout their votes.

Oppression (continued)

If the poor voted for
those who represented
their interests instead
of who corporations
plastered all over the
boob tube, we would have a
revolution unlike
anything seen before.

Democracy is a
radical idea.
It gives power to those
who have no money. A
healthy educated
nation benefits us
all. Will we ever see
anything like it here?

Jerry Falwell tried to
convince us the attacks
of 9/11 were
god's wrath for allowing
the homosexual
agenda to prevail.
If you read his bible —
the one about Jesus

not the one written by
the Jews — one could say the
tragedy punished us
for the way we treat our
poor. For Jesus said he
will judge nations by how
well they care for their weak
and sick. We won't do well.

F.I. Goldhaber

March 10, 2011

2011

*"Then they came for the trade unionists, and I
didn't speak out because I wasn't a trade union-
ist."*

Pastor Martin Niemöller

Last night the end started.
The only question: end of what?

For decades, the rich abused
the middle class, trying to take
us back to times of serfs,
peasants, and slaves. Union blood

bought us forty-hour work
weeks, two days off, pensions, health care
benefits. The middle
class expanded to include more

than merchants, small business
owners. The rich rebelled, taking
their jobs and paychecks to
China, India. The

U.S. prospers, but all
the money goes into only
a few pockets. They trashed
our economy, destroyed the

value of our homes, the
only asset most of us own,
and stole the taxes that
should have repaired roads, taught children,

28

protected our safety,
delivered quality health care
to us all. They monger
fear, set religious believers

against each other. Last
night they dropped all pretense of a
budget crisis, broke the
law, came for the trade unionists.

Last night the end started.
The only question: end of what?

Will the American
people finally wake up to
the outrageous, horrid,
parasitic travesties the
GOP perpetuated

on us all? Will they stop
allowing the GOP to
ignore/remove/destroy
our Constitutional rights? Or

did we hear the death knoll
of the Democratic party,
last night? Cash from corporate
America and the 400

who own more than millions
inundates the GOP with
ample funds buying votes
in Congress for more tax breaks and

March 10, 2011 (continued)

opportunities to
abuse what's left of the middle
class. Only the unions
have enough money to
fight back. Only the unions stand

between us and return
to a world run by dictators
and robber barons. The
ultra right-wing resorted to

lies and fabrications
against organizations that
register and recruit
minority, poor, and liberal

voters. Only unions
can compete against them. So the
big-money backers of
the Republican governor

have manufactured a
crises to take out the unions
in Wisconsin, using
public policy to destroy

their only rival. Should
their union busting succeed in
Wisconsin, Ohio,
Indiana, Pennsylvania,

they will come for the rest.
All the big political cash
to decide who wins and
loses elections will support

right-wing candidates. Bake
sales versus billionaires, what the
future of elections
will look like if we don't speak up.

Last night the end started.
The only question: end of what?

F.I. Goldhaber

Occupy America

2011

Young and old, jobless
and under employed
they stream downtown
to pitch their tents.

In the face of tear
gas and pepper spray,
false arrest and
imprisonment

they persevere. I'm
reminded of the
Révolution
Françaises, "To the

barricades!" Then the
students, impoverished
bourgeoisie, and
leftists banded

together to fight
for the principles
this young nation
introduced to

the world: Liberté,
égalité, and
fraternité.
We don't set fires

in the street. Instead,
we camp, we march, we
carry signs to
remind passers

by exactly who
the villains in this
conflict are: stock
brokers, bankers,

mega corps who have
bought all three branches
of the U.S.
government.

Unlike seventeen
eighty-nine, police
now throw the first
stones. Across the

country, leaders are
violating the
constitution
they have sworn to

protect, the one that
guarantees"the right
of the people
peaceably to

assemble." This is
where we must make our
stand. On the streets
and when we mark

Occupy America (continued)

our ballots next year.
They have the money.
We have the votes.
We're the ninety

nine percent. This: these
tents, these signs, is what
democracy
looks like today.

Choose to Occupy

2012

You seem to have vanished from public view,
but I know you whisper amongst yourselves.
Petty differences about process
divide you. Will you fritter away your
potential or will you burst forth armed with
the power of the 99 percent
and use the ballot box to take back our
country? Choose wisely, because the other
option's a bloody one. Revolution
is deadly and the cost in life is high.
You only need look to the Middle East
to see what could happen here. I know you've
lost faith in the process and, seeing what
it's produced, I understand. But, if you
resurrect the Occupy movement as
revolution, how many more will die?

F.I. Goldhaber

The Politics of Food

2013

Have you ever known hunger?
Have you ever chosen to
feed a child instead of eat?
When did you last know aching
emptiness that lasted days?
Millions of children in the
U.S. go hungry daily,
many more throughout the world
while billionaires steal the food
from their mouths to buy yachts, huge
mansions, fancy cars, private
jets, and their own Congressmen.
We subsidize the very
rich who eliminate jobs,
bust unions, ruin cities,
devastate education,
neglect infrastructure, and
take away your right to vote.
What they squander on one meal
at a fancy restaurant
could feed a poor family
of four for a month or more.

But, they begrudge the working
poor, the disabled, and the
unemployed whose jobs they stole,
a few hundred to spend at
the discount grocery store
to stop the rumbling in their
young children's empty bellies.
Forget about nutrition
that's an unaffordable
luxury available
only to those deemed worthy:
those who got rich taking from
the public coffers, building
their wealth with government-paid
subsidies and government
funded airports, roads, and ports.
They pocket their tax breaks and
complain about "handouts" and
nonexistent welfare queens.
Walk a few miles in a poor
man's shoes and skip eating for
a day or three. Try finding
a job when you're dizzy with
hunger. Give your meal to a
child who only eats at school
and goes without on weekends.

F.I. Goldhaber

Vote Them Wrong

2014

The pundits and pollsters
give us all the reasons
Republicans will steal
the Senate in '14.
Gerrymandering, lies
paid for by Koch brothers,
voter suppression laws,
and apathy of those
disenfranchised in so
many ways for so long.

You can change that. You have
power, you're endowed with
unalienable
rights as a citizen.
Use them. Register to
vote for November now.
And on that first Tuesday
Vote Them Wrong. Vote out Tea
Party malingerers,
ALEC's GOP pawns.
Ignore fabrications

that push the one percent's
agenda to create
laws eradicating
middle class, widening
income disparity.
Don't listen to campaign
rhetoric, follow the
money. Who pays for the ads
they bombard voters with?

Examine their voting
records. Ask who supports
them. Hyperbole will be
meaningless once voters
return them to office.
Isolated in the
capitol, federal
or state, secure knowing
they've two or more years to
wreak havoc on our lives.

Vote against them. If they
shut down governments, blocked
health care reform, busted
unions, or cut funds for
safety nets, bridges, roads,
education, science.
If they approved corporate
welfare and destruction
of the environment,
vote them out. Send them home.

Race Relations

Hate

2014

Billy said we didn't start the fire
But the world burns.
Muslims slaughter Christians in Iraq.
Yazidi flee.
Israelis and Gaza break truce once more.
ISIL fights Kurds.
Indians gang rape women daily.
Exiles swarm Chad.
Russia marches on Ukraine again.
Pakistan riots.
Azerbaijans kill Armenians.
Al-Qaeda plots.
Boko Haram kidnaps young girls, boys.
Syria bleeds.

And in the land of the free, cops kill.
Unarmed black men
executed by police daily.
Four black deaths in
one month capture the nation's concern.
But we don't learn
of so many more who die only
because their skin
color offended men of privilege.
Driving while black
in U.S., a capital offense.
Mothers teach sons
to raise hands, acquiesce ... but still
must bury them.

F.I. Goldhaber

Urban Warfare

2014

We arm police with military
surplus: flak jackets, gas masks, flash bangs,
riot shields, bayonets, machine guns,
APCs, helicopters, and tanks.
We created urban armies to
fight the misguided war on drugs which
devolved to hostilities against
citizens. Paramilitary
urban pacification forces
drill, waiting for opportunities
to attack, use their training, weapons.

The hammer sees every problem as
a nail. Soldiers see every person
who looks different as an enemy
combatant. Most officers are white.
People they routinely kill, tase, gas
have darker skin, kinky hair, accents.
White men traipse around stores brandishing
semi-automatic weapons while
unarmed black teens and mentally ill
boys holding knives lie bleeding to death
in streets, guilty only of black skin.

Tactics, terror, and trampling rights in
the best traditions of Stasi and
Cheka make folks fear calling for help.
Nine-year-olds handcuffed, taken to jail
for playground fights. Rape victims, treated
as criminals, assaulted again.
Kids suffering mental health crises
killed in front of parents. Mothers and
fathers who have committed no crime tased
to the ground while their children wail.
Trans women jailed for carrying condoms.

Protestors sprayed with tear gas, mace while
peacefully assembling. Homeowners
woken by cops breaking down their doors,
grenades exploding in their baby's
crib, because someone did not write an
alleged dealers' address correctly.
We fill private prisons with people
of color, enslaving them at a
buck an hour, robbing them and their
children of any hope of breaking
free of poverty's endless cycle.

Claiming title to "America's
Finest," police insist they're proud to
protect and serve. But, who exactly?
They rally 'round themselves, fighting off
any charges of violating
civil liberties, overstepping
authority. They lie to shield each
other, challenge every dismissal
in court. They thwart any effort to
restrain them, turning off cameras
designed to protect the public.

F.I. Goldhaber

Urban Warfare (continued)

Cops routinely torture innocents
to procure confessions. They ignore
evidence to obtain convictions.
How many years have those not guilty
served in prisons and sat on death row?
How many lives have courts stolen with
execution sentences based on
falsified evidence? If we do
not dismantle the military
machine patrolling our cities, the
blood shed tomorrow could well be yours.

Acknowledgements

The following poems have previously appeared in these publications: "Corporations," *Humdinger Literary E-zine*; "Winds of Change," "Occupy America," "Hate," and "Five Old White Men New," *New Verse News*; "Wallet Politics," "Lincoln was a Republican," and "Oppression," *Pairs of Poems*; "Separation of Church and State" and "March 10, 2011," *protestpoems.org*; "Trade Deficit," *Poetry for the Masses*.

www.ingramcontent.com/pod-product-compliance
Lightning Source LLC
Chambersburg PA
CBHW060052050426
42448CB00011B/2424